For Julia, with love —AM

For Rose and Nina —CL

And with so many thanks to Jo Gaskell

Text copyright © 2020 by Amanda McCardie
Illustrations copyright © 2020 by Colleen Larmour

First US edition 2021

Library of Congress Catalog Card Number 2021934569
ISBN 978–1–5362–1765–0

22 23 24 25 26 LEO 10 9 8 7 6 5 4 3 2

Printed in Heshan, Guangdong, China

This book was typeset in AnkeSans.
The illustrations were done in mixed media.

Candlewick Press
99 Dover Street
Somerville, Massachusetts 02144

www.candlewick.com

CANDLEWICK PRESS

Let's Play!

A Book About Making Friends

AMANDA McCARDIE   illustrated by COLLEEN LARMOUR

This is the story of Sukie and how she made friends.
It started when her family moved
and she had to go to a new school.

At first, she felt lonely, sad, and small . . .

Then some of her new classmates started being friendly.

One said hi to her during PE.

One passed her a hoop before they all got taken.

One helped her find her way when she was lost.

Each time, Sukie felt warm inside and wanted to be friendly back.

Now Sukie knew that friendliness was catching! So she smiled when she met a shy classmate by the coat pegs one morning.

The next time they met it was easier.

And the next time it was easier still.

Do you want to play?

Sukie and Joe were becoming friends.

When Sukie saw Poppy playing ball,
she plucked up her courage
and asked to join in.

Soon Poppy's friend Stan
joined in as well—and
friendship grew out of a game.

Sukie hoped all her friends would like one another. She brought them together many times, and soon she could see they did.

They were friends making friends with the friends of their friends!

But things weren't always easy for Sukie. One day, she asked a boy named Mikkel if she could help him with his puzzle, but Mikkel said no, he wanted to do it by himself. Sukie's skin felt crinkly with embarrassment.

She hurried away to find Poppy. For a while they played quietly, and then Sukie told Poppy what had happened. This kind of telling is called "confiding," which means that Sukie trusted Poppy—to be kind, to care how Sukie felt, and not to tell other people about it.

"Sometimes I want to play on my own, too," said Poppy.
They laughed, and the crinkly feeling faded away.

A few weeks later, Sukie's classmate Alex
made fun of her red hair.

12

Joe was ready to stand up for her right away.

He said calmly to Alex, "Stop being mean to Sukie."

Thanks, Joe.

READ

Everyone stopped laughing, even Alex. Her joke didn't seem very funny

after Joe called it mean. Joe was a brave, loyal friend that day.

13

One day, Sukie's class put on a special show for their parents in the gym—
but Joe rushed off before the show was over.

He felt silly, but his friends were there to support him.

Sukie found that she and her
friends were alike in lots
of ways.

They all enjoyed getting together,

playing

and laughing,

chatting,

being goofy,

and sharing lunch.

In other ways they were different. For instance, Stan didn't worry the way Sukie did.

Sukie was late sometimes, but Joe was almost always on time.

When Poppy was happy, she stood on her hands.

When Sukie was happy, she made people laugh.

And Sukie was happy. Not every minute, all the time—but warm and safely happy deep inside.

Knowing they had one another for support, Sukie and her friends

felt free to be open, to be themselves.

They grew closer every day.

AUTHOR'S NOTE

This book explores and celebrates some of the good things about friendship. Of course, friendships don't always look this way, and you might want to change some of these examples or add your own. That's fine!

This book doesn't show things going wrong between friends, even though sometimes they do. Instead, I wanted to focus on what it can look like when friendships go right.

Maybe you have friends in your life right now, or maybe you don't. Either way, I hope this book will help you reach out to the people around you and to think about what it really means to be a friend.

INDEX

* You'll find someone being kind on almost every page!